THE RISE OF GENDERQUEER

The Mineral Point Poetry Series

Tanka & Me	Kaethe Schwehn
My Seaborgium	Alicia Rebecca Myers
Fair Day in an Ancient Town	Greg Allendorf
My Tall Handsome	Emily Corwin
A Wife Is a Hope Chest	Christine Brandel
Black Genealogy	Kiki Petrosino
The Rise of Genderqueer	Wren Hanks
This Is Still Life	Tracy Mishkin
Life on Dodge	Rita Feinstein
Calf Canyon	Sarah McCartt-Jackson

The Mineral Point Poetry Series 7 · Kiki Petrosino, Editor

THE RISE OF GENDERQUEER

poems

Wren Hanks

Brain Mill Press
Green Bay, Wisconsin

Copyright © 2018 by Wren Hanks.
All rights reserved.

Published in the United States by Brain Mill Press.
Print ISBN 978-1-948559-09-6
EPUB ISBN 978-1-948559-12-6
MOBI ISBN 978-1-948559-10-2
PDF ISBN 978-1-948559-11-9

Cover photograph "Through the Veil" © H. Esmé Park.
Cover design by Oona Miller.

www.brainmillpress.com

The Mineral Point Poetry Series, number 7.
Published by Brain Mill Press, the Mineral Point Poetry Series is edited by Kiki Petrosino. In odd years, the series invites submissions of poetry chapbooks around a theme. In even years, the editor chooses a full collection.

for Jeanne

Contents

Foreword by series editor Kiki Petrosino   xi

The Ghost Incites a Genderqueer Pledge of Allegiance   1
My Ghost Sees Me Clearly as a Charred Tree Line   2
My Binder Is a ThunderShirt™   3
I'm not kissing girls who have to get / blitzed / to touch me   4
Who might rip the stuffing out of me,   5
Dear Daddy Pence, A List of My Luminous Indiscretions   6
Dear Daddy Pence, meet me at Olive Garden   7
Daddy Pence, when you kiss your wife is it like   8
The Rise of Genderqueer   9
In which I flirt with the cis girls at the reading like nothing matters   13
Spring Tells Me   14
The Rise of Genderqueer (Addendum 1)   15
The Rise of Genderqueer (Addendum 2)   16
The Rise of Genderqueer (Dream Log)   17
Grandmother, this fish tattoo is the only thing keeping me alive   18

Author's Acknowledgments   21
About the Author   23

"How I long to feel like southern gentry," Wren Hanks's speaker confesses in one of the earliest poems in this remarkable collection. It's a startling assertion to read in 2018, when so many of the American south's genteel monuments are coming down (or, at least, are scheduled to be moved elsewhere). What are we to make of this desire?

In *The Rise of Genderqueer*, references to "gentry" stand in as a kind of shorthand for the complex landscape of American masculinity. This realm—exclusionary, yet shimmering with ontological possibility for a speaker in transformation—is a place we might yearn to be in, if not of, a site we might, through these poems, seek to reclaim and restore. In this paradox, this unaccountable longing, is the project's appeal to the reader, to me and to you, and to anyone who's come of age in our culture's heady mix of patriarchy and pain, toxicity and ecstasy and contradiction. Hence, the "binder" is tool and torture device in these poems, as it symbolizes both the pain of physical transformation and the comforting "Thunder-Shirt" that pressurizes and consoles the body.

These poems are about desire. What the poet yearns for is not the masculinity that oppresses and taunts those purportedly "outside" its scope, but that *feeling* of ease within the body and within culture, that sense that the world you inhabit is one made for you. To be at home in one's body, to be at home in one's desire: such is the empowerment these poems seek. Poem by poem and line by astonishing line, Hanks builds a monument to that ineffable yearning—and then takes it apart, beautifully.

The Rise of Genderqueer proceeds via contradictory declarations of identity; the speaker is, by turns, gloriously confident in the body ("a boy with burning hair & the cerulean eyes of romance heroes") and wounded ("It's a mess inside me, ghost"). Reading the poems is a vivid, bruising journey. Many of the pieces are prose poems, which enact swift turns and emotional reversals before concluding with revelation ("It's the camera-ready red / this soldier's aiming for"). These poems produce a cumulative effect of disorientation in the reader, but lines like "walk with me into the garden" reveal that, at all times, we're in the hands of a guide who knows the fruits and quicksand of this particular Eden. We can trust this voice.

The Rise of Genderqueer is a garden, the sort where anything could grow from seed. The fragmentary phrase, "a psychologically healthy person," lifted from right-wing rhetoric meant to marginalize the transgender movement, becomes a stem onto which Hanks splices any number of flourishing lyrical branches. In these poems, the "psychologically healthy" person is, simultaneously, "a gelatinous animal under anyone's hands" and a locus of stability for the imagined beloved, "holding each other close / thinking we, in all of nature, are simple."

These poems are anything but simple. And it is within this complexity that Hanks fashions these gems of ever-changing colors. Read these poems, be shattered, get brave.

Kiki Petrosino
Editor, Mineral Point Poetry Series

THE RISE OF GENDERQUEER

The Ghost Incites a Genderqueer Pledge of Allegiance

Deny *girl* and the blood galaxies trailing it; there is a ghost in me who loves each egg, who won't let me throw up when I'm seasick from my period.

There is a ghost in me riffing on fertility & chocolate almonds. *We grow organs in pig ribs, ghost.* Surely swelling and blossoming are not the same.

Swelling's for an injured brain, a uterus drunk on the repetition of cells. I place my hand on my bound chest, pledge allegiance to the rashes and the scales, the fold and petal.

It's a mess inside me, ghost.

My Ghost Sees Me Clearly as a Charred Tree Line

I'm a cat in a surgery lab whose spine's been severed. I'm a boy with a vigorous hair flip. I'm a boy with burning hair & the cerulean eyes of romance heroes. You've stopped believing me now, but the ghost brings me Super Soakers to fight the neighbors, long since gendered & grown up. You've stopped believing me now, but I'm the one in the story with hands for eyes. The fir tree rustling with ash.

My brave ghost splits open at the chest, offers me a duelist's sword like we're in an episode of *Revolutionary Girl Utena*. You've stopped believing me now, but I'll cut a Midnight Supreme off your bustier. Toss my velvet hair and claim a scorched & empty win.

My Binder Is a ThunderShirt™

I need something stiff to breathe against like He-Man's armor. Like the anti-anxiety jacket I velcroed around shaking terriers when I was a dog walker. Back then, I zipped my hoodie to my neck. I wore Doc Martens & got muscle-skinny, riding the subway in giant headphones and licking cream cheese off my top lip. I ate whatever, I ate whatever, and my breasts shrank, but I moved to Texas and they came back, encouraged by fried avocado tacos I drizzled with two kinds of salsa.

My binder *applies gentle, constant pressure, similar to swaddling an infant*. My binder gives me the chest I didn't know I wanted, the chest of UT jocks in powder-washed polos. How I long to feel like southern gentry. But I'm a sleek dog yet, ThunderShirt tucked beneath my V-neck, holding me down.

I'm not kissing girls who have to get / blitzed / to touch me

I'm not I'm not I'm not / It's not true she wants / something different from me / than her boyfriend / Or it is / and that's hell too / she gets on her knees / on the dance floor / she presses her face against my hip / I'm supposed to pretend my body feels nothing / I know that / next time I'll say / my confusing body feels nothing / my traitor body feels nothing / put your hand in my jeans and see how much nothing I feel

I will / I'll say it / not / I'm wet & hard & still not real / enough / for you I won't say / I'm a good boy / enough-boy / a spit-curl-you-could-pull-when-I'm-sucking-your-clit boy / I'm dry I'll say / I'm chalk I'll say / pull off a limb and it'll grow back I'll say / but nothing / she tips back her head / the whiskey on her breath / the beet juice on her breath / like a sea star / I'm brainless / I won't I won't / move closer / her palm against my chest now / my sweating crushed ant chest now / just take another shot I'll say / just leaving me standing here I'll say / just go home with that girl / that boy I try / to say / before her drunk / her confident cis tongue / is in my mouth

Who might rip the stuffing out of me,

this dumb boy who wishes to be hot, this dumb boy who waits on deck for stolen endearments, one-winged termite crawling down his shirt, getting smashed by his lungs pushing in and out, breathing, it doesn't stop when the friend in front of you is beautiful, it doesn't stop when you can't kiss them.
I have swallowed sage, I have aftershaved and look how my legs glow, like a goat milked for spider silk I am precious, a thing to treasure. My glasses fog and this dumb boy sees the termites as portent, sees the salt only as an invitation to lick his friend's sighing mouth.

Dear Daddy Pence, A List of My Luminous Indiscretions

It's her mouth on my cock in a unisex bar stall / my hand squeezing his cock under the greasy table / it's my girlfriend on the marble countertop / while I'm breaking a wooden spoon / against her ass / Daddy, it's me in a car / at 16 / convincing a good Catholic boy / to put his hands on my breasts / it's that you think / I'm a dyke / when you see my shaved head / like definitions / will protect anyone / from me / Daddy, I'm coming / for your daughters / I'm coming for your sons / coming for the dog-whistle genders / in between / perhaps I am / the dog whistle / in between / Daddy Pence / don't wait up

Dear Daddy Pence, meet me at Olive Garden

We'll compare notes on nuptial bliss / on nights staring at Seven of Nine's tits / while our wives drink reasonable / thimbles of wine / on ironing shirts / (tomatoes off the vine, Daddy, / and garlic bread too) / on spitting our Crest into those sinks / rimmed / with cat hair / I'll take your hand / and ask you how long it's been / really / since one look / at a man's / brought your pulse up / I know the answer, already, Daddy / It's the camera-ready red / this soldier's aiming for

Daddy Pence, when you kiss your wife is it like

stars and stripes / your tongue an eagle's wing / no, wait, a talon / do you make her mute, daddy / the way you wanna make me / a silent statistic / de-transitioned with those / chewable / bubblegum hips / Daddy, were you ever / the beauty / on someone's bed / have you ever been / a fucking object

The Rise of Genderqueer

With language taken from the Family Research Council's "Understanding and Responding to the Transgender Movement" and "The Living Dead" by Peter Andrey Smith

1.

We have only begun to enter this "brave new world"   one that resists the genetic imprint found in every cell in the human body   Some convince others to see them as the other sex No one can change his or her sex   The DNA is marked clearly male or female
      the physical condition of their bodies   surgical alterations to their bodies
      involving as they do the amputation of healthy body parts   souls born into   healthy body parts   the state of being transgendered is extremely unstable
      an almost phobic lack of emotional and social flexibility
rejecting the gift of femaleness or maleness   some of their birth sex remains   their breasts removed   a Genderbread Person   an ontological insurgency   plastic and shaped by behavior   rebel against reality
walk with me into the garden   shine like a ribbon snake

A psychologically healthy person accepts the reality of his or her sexual identity
A psychologically healthy person accepts the reality of his or her sexual identity
A psychologically healthy person accepts the reality of his or her sexual identity

2.

A psychologically healthy person	*accepts*	*vines blooming on a rock wall*
Touch them and itch		*when their mouth on someone's clit*
is interchangeable		*I pretend I understand*
What it means to be human		*Putting oatmeal on poison ivy*
Welcome small scoops of danger		*Welcome the hollow place*
"Your chest feels solid" she says		*I am a gelatinous animal*
under anyone's hands		*Walk with me into the garden*
The animals can't line up by sex		*Because there are so*

If I were Adam I'd be so afraid of these divisions

3.

If I were Adam I'd be afraid my love of divisions
was a fetish for essentializing
(A psychologically healthy person accepts their kinks)
A psychologically healthy person crying, "I think I see God" when I tip them over the edge
But this is not about my topping skills, but this is about my topping skills
(Men of the FRC, I'd school you blow for blow)

A psychologically healthy person who thinks their chromosomes were sequenced at birth
Two psychologically healthy people holding each other close
thinking we, in all of nature, are simple

4.

A psychologically healthy person accepts their mortality

When a person dies the body begins to digest itself   *Will I be necro girl   necro boy*

Will it matter   mysterious organisms rapidly emerge

assemble on decomposing mammal flesh   *cuddled by the microscopic*

agents of death   those shorebound pirates lying in wait for the next shipwreck

There I'll be   belly turned oyster   Biologically normal persons of one sex cannot

become the other sex   *but   I / they can decompose*

the reality of what it means to be human   *is* healthy body parts

eventually   teeming with bugs   to rebel against reality

believing   the body rises again   *gender &* neuro-circuitry *intact*

the physical condition of *(our) (dead)* bodies   wizened strawberries   a slime trail

Instead of   one clear reproducible light

In which I flirt with the cis girls at the reading like nothing matters

like "love or die" is a tongue-in-cheek pin on my jacket and not the truth of it
hey, I've cultivated the veneer you're looking for
break me off like peanut brittle
cuz there's enough to go around
I like being something new (every girl, every time)
chick-fuzz cheeks, little voice-box that could
rasp in your ear

While I'm thinking about the trans girl who's actually killing me

her breath my breath
hating how she makes me feel like
nothing to be ashamed of
because what to do with that
what to do with hands on
(My god if they knew what it was to)
(really look at me)
(My god how scared I'd be)
(all the time)

Spring Tells Me

One day I will not hate myself for being a man.
It's enough that I want to kiss your lips down to mica.
It's enough that if I found a fly on your lips I'd eat it
because it touched your lips, it's obvious
I am not a girl. It's obvious now. Every turn of my head
spring tells me, *boy,
you are not a prince. You are a briar. Shh.* Every message
from you makes the sky go dark in my head over
the swan bed from the movie *Toys*,
but you're not animatronic, you're blood-rich—
lying there, your untied shoes, your sugar
in my system.

The Rise of Genderqueer (Addendum 1)

With language taken from "The Sacred Androgen: The Transgender Debate" by Daniel Harris

"One can no more change one's gender than one's species."
—Daniel Harris

Divest *me* of breasts and birth names & why not strip *me* of humanity.
Since nature was so maladroit, so incapable of fulfilling its responsibilities,
hand me a latchkey, a chivalrous rescue on the operating table.

I want to oxidize (*sans* chitchat), *sir Harris, I want to* get the inside out.
I'm willing to risk that *internal embargo*

on the likelihood the borders between the genders are more porous *than you or I know*,
more that an onslaught of papercuts *aimed at your (sorry) cisgender hands*
by any particular nest of snakes.

I'll never be denatured,

I am nature, walking past your mirror,
glory hanging *from each gutsy* redecorated cell.

The Rise of Genderqueer (Addendum 2)

With language taken from SB6 (Texas Legislature) and "The Mucus-Shooting Worm Snail That Turned Up in the Florida Keys" by Joanna Klein

a *psychologically healthy person* sees

the general diffusion of knowledge as potentially harmful

distracting environments   should be barred   (glues [their] home to hard surfaces)

to provide students access to restrooms, showers, and dressing rooms based on an individual student's internal sense of gender   is alarming

could potentially lead to boys and girls showering together

when using intimate facilities   a reasonable expectation of privacy
based on biological sex

is of the utmost priority and moral obligation of this state

where a person may be in a state of undress in the presence of another person
an   internal sense of gender would not seem so polite

regardless of whether the facility provides curtains or partial walls for privacy

(a sunken, retired naval ship   a limestone tube)

we're still not 100% sure where *they* are coming from

 nor how to contain

this kind of death-zone around them

The Rise of Genderqueer (Dream Log)

A psychologically healthy person is a composite

of dreams   Banded parasites spilling from a hole in his breast

Warts shaped like doors   tub full of ants grasping a sponge

*   In these dreams he's a woman*

still   & no one can tell him when this will end

While kissing his middle school crush

in an abandoned gas station

She'll wipe his charcoal stubble off

*   to reinstate the smoothness underneath*

Grandmother, this fish tattoo is the only thing keeping me alive

on days when I want to hurt my wrist but not these blue specks of a past when I slept with a man, kept a tank of withering plants and these reasonable schools always circling. The cherry shrimp molting, dying, I was always traveling to Chinatown for crystal invertebrates. Grandmother, I am a slut but you know that, prescient as your ghost is with its bird-claws dug into my shoulders. A slut who can't take off his clothes in the best of situations. I remember how magnetic you were in pictures—how even in black and white I could tell your lipstick was the crimson you could crush a man under, leave his collar dirty, leave a temporary fossil record. You lost that love for your body, but I've never loved mine to begin with. If I could mourn myself. If I could mourn myself the way I mourned the tetra whose belly ruptured before my eyes, maybe I could cut into my own belly like a block of cheese. You, grandmother, would understand not dying is an active state, where I vibrate with world-bits in my legs and chest and wrists. Crystal shrimp. Pulling J's hair. Shredded potatoes I pick off my shirt and eat.

Author's Acknowledgements

Grateful acknowledgement is made to the publications where individual poems from this manuscript have appeared, sometimes in earlier versions:

Best New Poets 2016, *decomP*, *Emerge: 2016 Lambda Fellows Anthology*, *Heavy Feather Review*, *Gigantic Sequins*, *Jellyfish Magazine*, *Permafrost*, and *The Wanderer*.

About the Author

Wren Hanks is the author of *Prophet Fever* (Hyacinth Girl Press) and co-editor of *Curious Specimens* (Sundress Publications), an anthology of the strange and uncanny. A 2016 Lambda Emerging Writers Fellow, his work appears or is forthcoming in *Best New Poets*, *Foglifter*, *Gigantic Sequins*, *Waxwing*, and elsewhere. He lives in Brooklyn with his wife.

www.ingramcontent.com/pod-product-compliance
Lightning Source LLC
Chambersburg PA
CBHW051334110526
44591CB00026B/2998